The NEW BANNER BOOK

written and illustrated by
Betty Wolfe

MOREHOUSE PUBLISHING

Procedure and Contents

ST. MATTHEW

Getting Started
using banners

where when how why

Places
church, parish hall, narthex, classroom, office, home, entry hall—in fact, any space that needs a spot of color

Times and occasions
Seasons: Christmas, Epiphany, Lent, Easter, Pentecost
Celebrations: weddings, baptisms, confirmations, bar mitzvahs
Special events: festivals, pageants

As hangings
against the wall, from a pole, from the ceiling, as a divider, on the lectern, pulpit, or altar

Carried
in a procession: entry, gospel, offertory, wedding, or festival

Purposes
to produce a mood or set the stage for a specific event; to add color, beauty, and meaning to an event; to define an area; to identify a place or organization, as a memorial, a gift, or a permanent work of art

the FIRST decision
how BIG?

The **size** will be determined by:

♦ the size of the room
♦ the height of the ceiling
♦ the available wall space

How it will be used:

If the banner is to be carried, it must be a comfortable **size** for the person who carries it.

Processional banners should be two-sided.

the SECOND decision
what SHAPE?

Shape is primarily a matter of proportion—the ratio of height to width, that is, tall and thin, short and wide, etc. In general, this is determined by where and how the banner will be used.

Examples: square (1 x 1), rectangular, horizontal or vertical, (1 x 1, 1½ x 1, 1 x 1½, 1 x 2, 1 x 3, and so on)

Another shape may be added to the bottom of a basic rectangular shape.

The dominant horizontals and verticals of all of the above shapes relate well to architecture, but any shape that will hang is possible. Experiment with: (a) panels hanging side by side, (b) twisted or draped shapes, (c) layered shapes, or (d) inverted triangles.

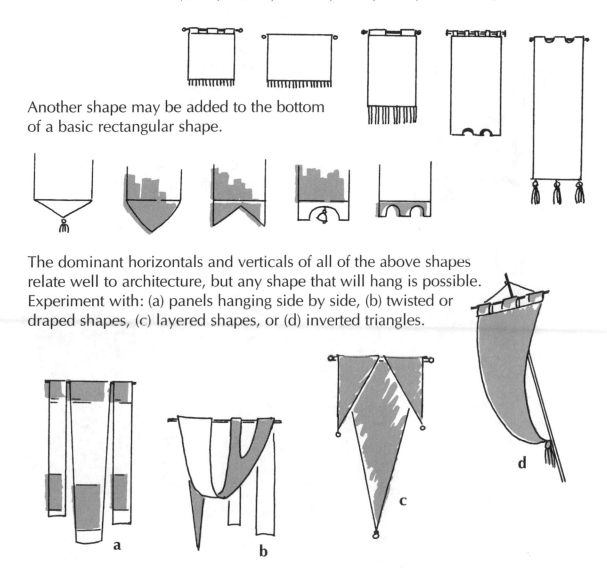

the THIRD decision
the MESSAGE

In addition to being a decorative hanging, **a banner speaks.**

The very nature of fabric hanging loosely, moving with every breath of air, free to flow, to sway, to flap, speaks of freedom, of motion, of aliveness.

what can a BANNER say and do?

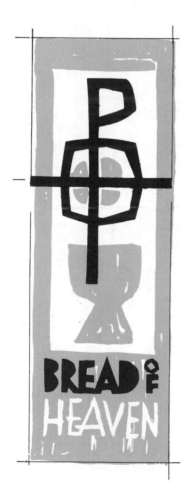

produce a mood, an atmosphere of welcome, joy, solemnity, peace, quiet, excitement, celebration, thoughtfulness, devotion, inspiration

proclaim hope, victory, praise, good news, a message, a slogan, a motto, a challenge, a prayer, glories of the past, action in the present, visions for the future

affirm the faith, an ideal, the truth

identify an event, a group, a season, an organization

how does a banner *SPEAK?*

through:

words

See pages 8–18.
a combination of
LETTERS

symbols

See pages 19–32.
SIGNS
FIGURES (people shapes)
a STORY/EVENT

color

See pages 33–36.

design

See page 41.
TWO KINDS

the MESSAGE through WORDS

In this age of literacy, the most universally understood symbols are **words.** Words may be the only symbols on a banner. Often a thought that must be proclaimed through words speaks more emphatically without additional symbols.

Designing with **letter forms** alone can be as challenging a problem as arranging other kinds of shapes or symbols. The resulting banner can be rich, colorful, and decorative.

Study the letters on the following pages to help you create an attractive hanging.

Often a banner expressing an idea through shapes and symbols will be made more meaningful through the addition of a word or phrase as a key to its interpretation.

Examples: JOY, PEACE, PAX, LOVE, REJOICE, ALLELUIA, SHALOM, AMEN

Banners for saints, seasons, historical characters, or groups may be identified with a name.

Examples:
- ST. PETER
- ST. MARY'S CHURCH
- CATHEDRAL OF ST. JOHN
- ST. HILDA'S GUILD
- TRINITY PREP

- THE WESLEY CLASS
- THE BELL RINGERS
- FEAST OF LIGHTS
- REDEEMER CHURCH
- ST. CECELIA CHOIR

For banners with a religious theme, the Scriptures, hymns, psalms, liturgies, and canticles are sources of meaningful words. The phrases are countless, the translations many.

Examples:
- Glory Be to God
- Glory to God
- Thy Kingdom Come
- Venite Adoremus
- Bread of Heaven
- Cup of Salvation
- Jesus Is Lord

- God Is Love
- Christ Is Risen
- Read, Mark, Learn
- Kyrie Eleison
- Do This
- One in the Lord

- One Lord, One Faith, One Baptism
- O Come, O Come, Emmanuel
- Love One Another
- Praise the Lord

SAMPLES
of various type styles

SOME THINGS TO DO to make lettering easier and fun

1. Observe the great variety of letter forms used in printing and advertising. Become aware of their basic shapes, proportions, and individual characteristics.

2. Make a **collection** of letters from magazines and newspapers. Include both capital and small letters, roman and italic. **Bold** letters (with thick strokes) will be especially helpful. Also include samples of **condensed** (narrow), **expanded** (wide), and **italic** letters. Notice the small variations in form that give each typeface its particular style. Look at the width of strokes—where they are thick or thin. Observe the spacing of letters within the word.

3. Following the directions on page 10, make a chart of **CAPS.** This is especially helpful if you plan to work with young people or other groups making banners.

miracles **it** Surprise power **map** wood **out** bouquet created it. **fort** garden for you bean **South** scratch *Italian*

9

the MESSAGE through WORDS

Words are made of **letters.** There are two basic kinds of letters:

1. capital letters (CAPS)—uppercase, either sans serif or with serifs
2. small letters—lowercase, either sans serif or with serifs

CAPS

Below is a chart of bold sans serif caps arranged according to standard widths.
Notice: The letters are all the same height, but they vary in width.

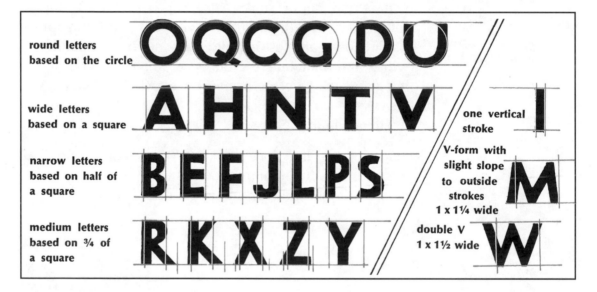

important:

♦ In sans serif letters, the ends of all straight strokes are square.

♦ The center horizontal stroke of the **E** and **H** is slightly above center.

♦ On the **A** and **F**, the center stroke is below center.

♦ The vertical of the **G** is its distinguishing feature.

♦ The **I** and **J** have no cross pieces at top or bottom.

♦ The diagonals of the **K** and **R** hook onto the upright.

♦ The bottoms of the **V**, **W**, and **N** are almost points. Also, the "V" of the **M** touches the bottom letter line, and the mid-point of the **W** touches the top letter line.

♦ The center stroke of the **E** and **F** is as wide as the top stroke.

small LETTERS

An alphabet of small (lowercase) letters can be designed from four basic shapes.

These forms are:

   ○   1 — the *o* form

   ⌐   2 — the curve of the *n*

   i l   3 — the straight line as in *i* and *l*

   /   4 — the diagonal lines

Combine them to make all of the lowercase letters.

o   **abcdegopq s**   } letter line

                           <   spaces between letter lines for descending and ascending strokes

⌐   **ahnmrfu**

i/   **ijlt kvwxyz**   } letter line

Notice that only the **b, d, h, f, l,** and **k** are tall letters with ascending strokes the height or higher than the caps. The **t** is shorter than the other tall letters and the cross bar is at the height of the letter line. Note the height of the upper diagonal stroke of the **k.**

   The **g, p, q, j,** and **y** have descending strokes that go below the letter line.

notice

In the letters at the right, changing the shape and slant of the three basic shapes will change the style of the alphabet. Try expanding, slanting, joining, and adding serifs to make your own lowercase alphabet.

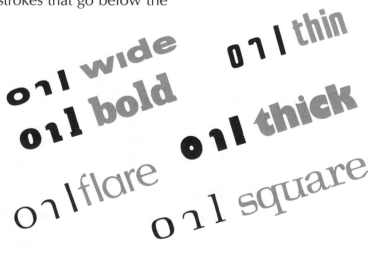

oⁿl wide

oⁿl thin

oⁿl bold

oⁿlflare

oⁿl thick

oⁿl square

PATTERNS
for LETTERS

Here is an easy way to cut your own patterns.

Cut strips of paper the height of the letters in your banner design.

Referring to the chart on page 10, mark off the width of each letter in the words of your banner. Try chalk.

If your patterns turn out to be too large or small, reduce or enlarge them on a copy machine and save lots of time.

Within these widths, draw the letters. Think about what will be **cut away** in order to leave the bold letter forms required for a banner.

Cut apart and cut out each letter. **Notice** that the straight tops and bottoms are already cut. Since these are patterns, cut through to get inside a letter.

Mechanical (measured) regularity in width of letter strokes or of duplicate letters is not necessary—in fact, it gives a sterile look. These letters have a slight flare. See page 16.

For *O's* and other round letters, cut the strip a fraction wider in order to compensate for the optical illusion that will make these letters appear too short.

In most banners the strokes of cutout letters should be **bold**, not thin.

a bonus
These letters are excellent for posters and bulletin boards.

Once you know the basic proportions of letters, you are free to have fun with them. In other words, once you understand the rules, you can break them.

some variations

Make extended strokes—if they enhance the design.

AEFGHJKLNVS

Overlap an occasional letter *if* it fits. Some will fit inside each other easily, or touch comfortably. Don't force them.

LORD   IT HALT

Vary the width of the strokes.

FUN   TALES

Bounce letters up and down a very little, or stagger slightly. Either technique will give a less mechanical, more vibrant effect.

DANCE   TILT

Try leaving the centers solid.

ABCDKMOPRW

Add serifs. See page 16.

Do not do any of these unless they enhance the design. Fancy or clever letters are not more beautiful, nor more easily read.

for the PROFESSIONAL look

SOME DOs AND DON'Ts for arranging letters and words

spacing

BETWEEN LETTERS
Pack the letters close together within each word.

Some combinations of letters can be permitted to touch each other.

BETWEEN WORDS
Between words, leave room for an *O*.

BETWEEN LINES
Normally the space between lines of letters should be narrow, almost touching.

emphasis
to emphasize an **important word,** use one large letter or large letters in that one **word.**

but
do not capitalize the first letters of a line of capital letters.

COMPACT
not S C A T T E R E D

FOR○A○CIRCLE
a○circle

like: not:

SINGLE SPACING ON THE TYPEWRITER

DOUBLE SPACING

OR EVEN WORSE

TRIPLE SPACING

GOD IS LOVE
GOD IS LOVE

FIRST LETTERS OF CAPITAL LETTERS

always arrange the letters
HORIZONTALLY

The WORDS are to be read; therefore, they ought to be **legible at a glance.**

1. When space is short, arrange a word in syllables.

2. Arrange words as though within a rectangle **if** they fit without forcing.

3. Arrange lines of words blocking them either to the left or right margin, or both when possible.

4. Group words as if contained within a circle or elliptical shape.

5. When the design demands a vertical or a diagonal, turn the **entire word.**

SYL-
LA-
BLES

LIKE
THIS

GO
TEAM

in a
shape
like a
box

LET
THE
SUN
SHINE
IN

TURN

UP HILL

Do **not** arrange words vertically or on the diagonal. Diagonal margins carry the eye to the corner of the composition, destroying the basic rectangular shape of the banner design.

not down like

not CHINESE

not DIAGONAL

DO
NOT
ARRANGE
LIKE
THIS

SERIFS

CAPS

The caps in the chart on page 10 are bold sans serif letters, i.e., letters without decorative endings.

The addition of the serif changes the style of the letters.

In addition to thick and thin strokes and small variations in proportions, the design of the serif accounts for the many styles of letters used in printing.

Notice that there are almost never serifs on the top of *A*, or on the pointed bottoms of *M*, *N*, *V*, and *W*.

SQUARE SERIFS

CURVED SERIFS

TRIANGULAR SERIFS

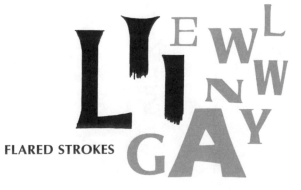

FLARED STROKES

ALPHABETS

These letters are **OPTIMA BOLD,** 36 point, CAPS (uppercase)

ABCDEFGHIJKLMN
OPQRSTUVWXYZ

These letters are **optima bold,** 36 point, small (lowercase)

abcdefghijklmn
opqrstuvwxyz

This style of letters is called **UNCIAL** and is adapted from medieval handwritten letter forms and designed **bold** to be appropriate for cutting from fabric. The letters tend to be rather elegant and are spaced very close together, sometimes touching.

AABCDEFFGGh
IJJKKLLmNOPQ
RSTUVVWXYYZ

The letters below are lowercase, designed for banners. There are no caps.

abcdefghijklmn
opqrstuvwxyz

Suggestion: Enlarge the letters on a copy machine. Although there is no standard height for letters on banners, they should be at least 2½" to 3" tall.

For more formal or traditional style banners, use UNCIAL or VERSAL letters. The forms below are adapted from medieval pen letters for cutout letters.

Characteristics of

1. Round forms are used for *D, E, H, M, N, P, T, U, and W.*

2. The vertical strokes are thick; the horizontals are thin.

3. The ascending strokes of *D, H, K,* and *L* go above the letter line. The descending strokes of *J, P, Q,* and *Y* go below the letter line.

Characteristics of

VERSAL

These are based on roman letter forms (page 10), but they were handwritten letters, and each scribe developed his own style and proportions.

1. The vertical strokes are thick; the horizontal strokes thin.

2. All strokes flare slightly toward the ends.

3. There is a slight bow on the round strokes.

the MESSAGE through SYMBOLS

Christian symbols, like letters, are simple forms, not realistic pictures of objects. The meanings of the symbols, like letters, must be learned. This is not a part of public-school learning; some are understood by association, some are picture like. Actually, many are letters from the Greek alphabet.

To their advantage, the meaning and basic forms of symbols are the same no matter what language one speaks. They are universal signs. Many Christian symbols date back to the first centuries after Christ, while Old Testament symbols are older than the writings of the Scriptures.

When natural forms (birds, animals, plants, people) and man-made objects (buildings, tools, and so on) are depicted, they should be symbolic, that is, simple, conventionalized and two-dimensional.

The symbols on the following pages may be put together in many combinations in order to tell a story or proclaim the **message.**

EXAMPLES

CROSS or CHI RHO combined with

- a FISH = salvation through Christ
- a CROWN = God's reign
            = Christ the King
- NAILS = Passion of Christ
- FIVE DOTS = five wounds of Christ
- THREE CIRCLES = Christian marriage
- DESCENDING DOVE = grace
- DOVE WITH WATER = baptism (of Christ)
- ALPHA and OMEGA AΩ = God's eternity
- STAR OF DAVID = old and new Covenant

SYMBOLS
sketches, meanings, and descriptions

CROSSES—The Christian symbol = sacrifice, God's love, salvation. Crosses **always** stand upright in their original position.

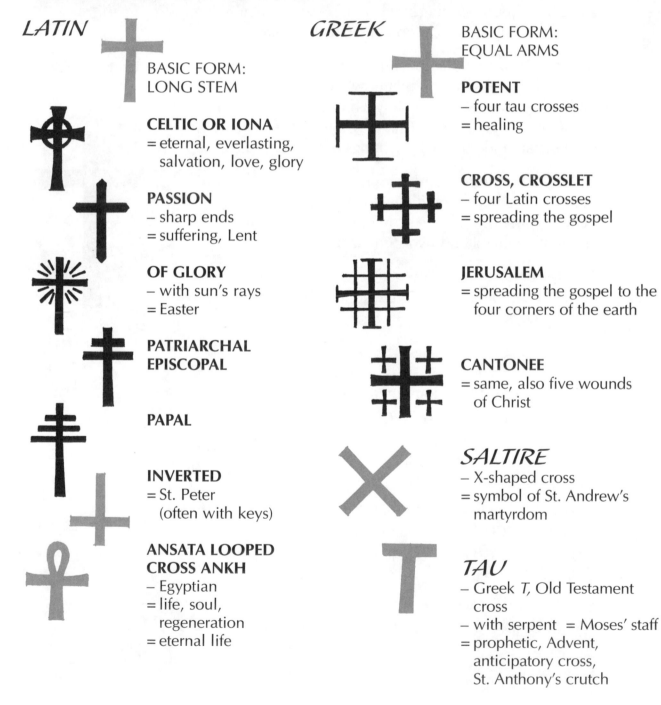

LATIN

BASIC FORM:
LONG STEM

CELTIC OR IONA
= eternal, everlasting,
salvation, love, glory

PASSION
– sharp ends
= suffering, Lent

OF GLORY
– with sun's rays
= Easter

**PATRIARCHAL
EPISCOPAL**

PAPAL

INVERTED
= St. Peter
(often with keys)

**ANSATA LOOPED
CROSS ANKH**
– Egyptian
= life, soul,
regeneration
= eternal life

GREEK

BASIC FORM:
EQUAL ARMS

POTENT
– four tau crosses
= healing

CROSS, CROSSLET
– four Latin crosses
= spreading the gospel

JERUSALEM
= spreading the gospel to the
four corners of the earth

CANTONEE
= same, also five wounds
of Christ

SALTIRE
– X-shaped cross
= symbol of St. Andrew's
martyrdom

TAU
– Greek *T,* Old Testament
cross
– with serpent = Moses' staff
= prophetic, Advent,
anticipatory cross,
St. Anthony's crutch

20

SYMBOLS
THE CHRISMON and OTHER MONOGRAMS

CHI RHO = CH R   (Greek) monogram for Christ.

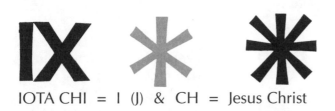

IOTA CHI = I (J) & CH = Jesus Christ

IHS IHC  **IHS**

IOTA ETA SIGMA = I (J), E (H), and S (or C) = JES in Greek IHS or IHC

AΩ AW AΩ

ALPHA and OMEGA = A Ω, the beginning and the
end, or eternity. Use with a cross or a symbol for Christ.

NIKA = victor or victory over death
        through the cross

IC XC = IOTA SIGMA JS = JESUS
      = CHI SIGMA CS = CHRISTUS

INRI

INRI = Jesus of Nazareth, King (Rex) of the Jews;
       the sign over the cross at the crucifixion

SYMBOLS

NIMBUS – circle of light
HALO = holy, sanctified, a saint
– triradiant = divinity

CROSS = orb represents the world,
AND the cross = triumph of the Savior
ORB over the sins of the world;
Christ's conquest and reign;
gospel in the world; Epiphany

CIRCLE = everlasting, eternal, wholeness, unity
– two close, or interlaced =
marriage or family
– with cross, Christ symbol,
or dove = Christian marriage

TRIANGLE – Holy Trinity
– in a circle = unity of the
Holy Trinity

TREFOIL – three interlacing circles = Holy Trinity
– with circle = eternal, Trinity
in unity

FLEUR-DE-LIS – a conventionalized lily
= Holy Trinity, the Annunciation,
the Blessed Virgin Mary, purity
= Christ's humanity

LILY = St. Gabriel, Archangel, Annunciation
= Easter; suggests life from death as
bloom comes from bulb

SUN = prophetic symbol for Jesus
= Sun of Righteousness

MOON = the Blessed Virgin Mary;
her glory is in the reflection of the Sun

SYMBOLS

STARS = light, a part of God's creation
 – four points = cross form
 – five points = star of Bethlehem, Epiphany,
   five books of Moses
 – six points = star of David
 – seven points = gifts of the Holy Spirit
 – eight points = regeneration, rebirth, baptism
 – nine points = fruits of the Spirit

MENORAH – seven-branch candlestick = Old Testament = worship

FIRE FLAMES – tongues of fire = Pentecost, Holy Spirit
 seven = seven gifts of the Holy Spirit
 = the presence of God, as in burning bush, the pillar of fire

CANDLES = light, Jesus, light of the world, the mystery of the Incarnation
 wax = Jesus' human body; wick = his soul; flame = his divinity
 two = humanity and divinity of Jesus
 four = Advent
 seven = gifts of the Spirit, sacraments

PASCAL CANDLE – with five nail marks = Christ's death and resurrection; when burning, his risen presence in our midst; the Easter candle

LAMP = wisdom, knowledge
 – sanctuary lamp = presence of Christ in the Holy Sacrament

DOVE – descending = the Holy Spirit
 – with triradiant halo = divinity, third person of Holy Trinity
 – with olive branch = peace, forgiveness, Noah

SYMBOLS

SCALLOP = Holy Baptism, pilgrim
SHELL – three = St. James the Greater

MITRE = the Episcopacy, bishop, apostolic ministry
– two points = tongues of fire of Pentecost
– two streamers = living water

CROOK = shepherd, the Good Shepherd, nativity of Jesus, bishop, bishop's crozier, the Episcopate

SHIP = the church, a cross or the chi rho being the mast = Christ, the captain

WATER = Holy Baptism, cleansing, washing, purification
– three drops = Holy Trinity in baptism

ARK and RAINBOW = God's promise, covenant with man

KEY = St. Peter
= keys of the kingdom, repentance, absolution, sacrament of penance, forgiveness

JUG – of oil = healing, holy unction
– six of water = marriage at Cana

CHALICE and HOST = bread and wine, bread of life, cup of salvation, Holy Communion, Lord's Supper, the Mass, eucharistic worship, Maundy Thursday
= the new covenant
– with symbol of Christ = his presence

CHALICE – with passion cross = Gethsemane
– with serpent = St. John, apostle and evangelist

WHEAT and GRAPES = Last Supper, Lord's Supper
= fruits of the earth

SYMBOLS

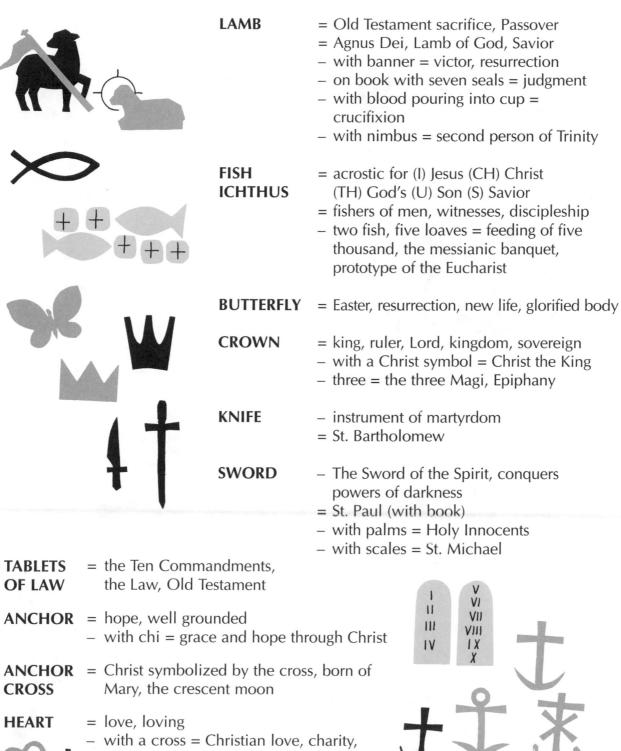

LAMB = Old Testament sacrifice, Passover
= Agnus Dei, Lamb of God, Savior
– with banner = victor, resurrection
– on book with seven seals = judgment
– with blood pouring into cup =
crucifixion
– with nimbus = second person of Trinity

**FISH
ICHTHUS** = acrostic for (I) Jesus (CH) Christ
(TH) God's (U) Son (S) Savior
= fishers of men, witnesses, discipleship
– two fish, five loaves = feeding of five
thousand, the messianic banquet,
prototype of the Eucharist

BUTTERFLY = Easter, resurrection, new life, glorified body

CROWN = king, ruler, Lord, kingdom, sovereign
– with a Christ symbol = Christ the King
– three = the three Magi, Epiphany

KNIFE – instrument of martyrdom
= St. Bartholomew

SWORD – The Sword of the Spirit, conquers
powers of darkness
= St. Paul (with book)
– with palms = Holy Innocents
– with scales = St. Michael

**TABLETS
OF LAW** = the Ten Commandments,
the Law, Old Testament

ANCHOR = hope, well grounded
– with chi = grace and hope through Christ

**ANCHOR
CROSS** = Christ symbolized by the cross, born of
Mary, the crescent moon

HEART = love, loving
– with a cross = Christian love, charity,
Christ's compassion

25

SYMBOLS

CROWN OF THORNS	
SPEAR	
THREE NAILS	
SCOURGE	
DICE	= Passion symbols
MONEY BAG	– with thirty coins = Judas, betrayal – three = St. Matthew
SHIP	= mission, St. Jude, apostle, Paul's voyages
SAW	= St. James the Less
BROKEN CHAIN	= forgiveness, freedom from sin and slavery, reconciliation

BOOK = Holy Scripture, Word of God,
the Gospel

HAND = of God = omnipotence,
Creator; (often with three fingers
extended = blessing)

EYE = God the Father, omniscience;
often in triangle or circle and
with triradiant cross

APPLE = temptation, sin

TREE = tree of life, "I am the vine,"
root of Jesse

**PALM
BRANCHES** = triumph, victory, Palm Sunday

an easy way to make your own PATTERNS

...or how to DESIGN a SYMBOL

1. Cut a paper shape to the size of the area that the symbol is going to fill in the banner. See the square, rectangle, circle, and triangle below.

2. Fold the shape in half or quarters.

3. Draw the outline of half of the symbol, full-size, remembering that the center is at the fold.

4. Cut it out. Open it up. This will work for any symmetrical shape.

   Examples: Greek cross forms, chalice and host, shell, butterfly, anchor, heart, and open book.

5. Cut patterns from scrap paper or old newspapers. Cut many patterns until the shape is pleasing and the size right for your banner.

another way to DESIGN and make SYMBOLS and other SHAPES

1. Cut strips of paper of varying widths. Use a paper cutter if one is available.

2. Cut off lengths from the strips to make the pattern for any shape made from straight lines.

3. Glue or tape the strips together to form the patterns.

GEOMETRIC shapes

The general silhouette of many things, both man-made and natural forms, can be expressed in geometric shapes.

Cut out squares, rectangles, triangles, circles, and half circles and put them together to make patterns for the design units of the banner.

Notice the basic shapes of the symbols on page 30.

Look at natural* and man-made
objects; become aware of their
basic shapes, or look for objects
that are basically a
geometric shape.

*from nature: leaves, pods,
flowers, seeds, trees, birds,
insects, reptiles

making designs and patterns

Another way to design and make patterns of symbols and shapes:

From within a shape, cut a design. Use either the cutout or the negative (or both) in your banner design.

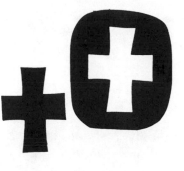

cut and flip

From the edge of a shape such as a rectangle, cut a shape, flip it, and then cut again. You might create an interesting border.

You may be surprised by the sense of rhythm you produce by this trick!

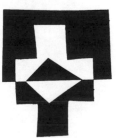

more suggestions

From a given shape, **cut** and **spread** or **expand** or **explode** to create a rhythmic repetition. Cutting a shape is often easier than drawing it. Experiment.

the MESSAGE expressed in COLOR

The dominant color scheme of a banner will be determined by its use and location. The wall color, amount of light, season, and basic theme are factors that will help decide the choice of color.

the effect

With this in mind, decide on the **general effect** the banner is to project.

Examples:
- jewel-like
- bright
- bold
- earthy
- subdued
- muted
- light
- striking
- vivid

background

For background fabrics, see page 46.
For amount to purchase, see page 47.

Having decided on the size and shape of your banner (pages 4 and 5), decide on the color of the background and purchase the fabric. See the next page for suggestions.

appliqués

Color can be discussed academically, and rules can be stated; however, the final choice should be what looks best.

All bright colors are wonderful and look right together. Put them side by side and see if they are friendly. Appliqués must be either *lighter* or *darker* than the background. Use lots of closely related colors, for example, red, red-orange, orange, yellow-orange, and light olive green; or try blue-green, aqua, blue, and blue-violet.

Black behind bright colors really sets them off.

For skin tones, find fabric close to the color of brown wrapping paper.

play it by EYE

Make a collection of **fabric** samples, scraps, and remnants, especially of bright, solid colors.

Lay these samples on the background fabric. Select the ones that look best together and produce the right effect. Forget what has been said about "never put X color next to Y color"—try every combination.

Take away any color that looks faded beside the others or is too vivid to blend. Often it is surprising to find which colors do look right together. **Play it by eye,** be daring, and keep in mind the basic effect the colors are to project.

There is no such thing as an ugly color. However, there are less-than-beautiful combinations. Become aware of color in everything you see.

suggestions for backgrounds

The background need not be the color of the season, but rather something that enhances the building in which it will be used, and celebrates the day.

- ◆ OFF-WHITE: *Never* dead white, but creamy white, ivory, oyster white, or very light beige or gray tones are all acceptable. Good in a dark building.

- ◆ RED: Bright red, crimson, vermilion, cranberry, and red-orange

- ◆ BLUE: Medium bright, ultramarine, cobalt

- ◆ GOLD: In paints/pigments, this is called yellow ochre. It is a "dull yellow," but really very bright, light, and elegant. An excellent background.

- ◆ NEUTRAL: The color of natural linen/beige. Oatmeal is often a good backing for bright appliqués.

- ◆ GREEN: Bright greens, kelly green, light olive green, even yellow-green are possibilities. It depends on the building.

- ◆ VIOLET/PURPLE: Less frequently used because a dark color by nature.

- ◆ RED, BLUE, GOLD, AND OFF-WHITE ARE FAVORITES

seasonal colors

The traditional seasonal colors for the Christian seasons of the church year:
- ◆ Advent: violet (purple)
- ◆ Christmas season: gold or white
- ◆ Epiphany celebration: gold or white
- ◆ Season of Epiphany: green
- ◆ Lent: violet, black for Passion
- ◆ Easter season: white or gold
- ◆ Feast of Pentecost: red
- ◆ Season after Pentecost: green

OTHER TRADITIONS
- ◆ Advent: a rich, bright blue, with pinks and light violet, maybe gold
- ◆ Lenten array: off-white/oatmeal with dark blood red and black or brown (This is pre-Reformation Anglican use. It is much subdued from the rich purple traditionally in use during this penitential season.)
- ◆ Palm Sunday and Holy Week: dark red

contrast

In order for the symbols, words, and shapes in a banner design to show up, they must be:
lighter or
darker than the background,
and probably a different color from the background... this is **important.**

notice

Bright yellow is always light, while bright purple is dark. Within this range from yellow to purple are all the values of the other colors.

what's in a NAME?

Keep in mind that the color-name **yellow,** for example, means many shades:

dark yellow	(olive-green)	
medium	(gold, khaki)	} = value
or light	(pale-yellow)	
bright	(yellow)	
dull	(green-gold)	} = intensity
warm	(yellow-orange)	
cool	(yellow-green)	} = hue

or nearly neutral, that is, almost black, white, or grey.

This is true with all colors—there is light red (pink), dark red (maroon), bright red (crimson), warm red (vermilion), dull red, red-orange, red-violet, and every shade in between.

suggestion

Become aware of the great variety of shades of colors. Notice those combinations that appeal to you—in advertising, printed fabrics, interior design, and so forth.

related COLORS

Colors next to each other on the color wheel are closely related. Like members of a family, they look somewhat alike and seem to go together because they have a common parent. For example, violet (purple), red-violet, red-orange, and orange all have some red in them. They are called *analogous* colors.

color intensity

Almost all bright colors get along well together. They are vibrant and enhance each other. This is especially true of analogous colors.

However, dull colors seem out of place with bright ones. They are cancelled out and become almost no color. They look faded. Therefore, mixing bright and dull colors usually makes an unfavorable combination. However, grayed colors blend and bring out each other when used *together*.

opposite colors

Colors opposite each other on the color wheel, such as green and red are called complementary colors. Blue and orange, and yellow (gold) and violet are other examples of complementary colors. They contrast too strongly to be used in equal amounts and tend to vibrate unpleasantly.

However, a small spot of a complementary color, for example, a touch of green in an area of mostly reds or a small bit of orange in a field of blue, will create a needed accent.

STITCHERY

The process described in this book is that of **appliqué**, that is, cutting shapes from cloth and applying them to a background fabric. Compatible additions to appliqué are creative stitchery and crewel embroidery. However, it is important that they be in character and proportion to the bigness and boldness of the appliqué technique, **not** the addition of realistic fussy detail.

Stitchery may be used to give **texture** to areas of flat color on cutouts or background areas. Use large French knots, straight stitch, or cross-stitch.

To **outline** or create a **linear** design, use a chain stitch, cross-stitch, buttonhole, stem stitch, or couch stitch.

To couch on the sewing machine:

Draw a light line where you want to stitch a line. Using the largest zigzag stitch, hold the yarn through the presser foot and stitch, following the line you have drawn. Do not glue the yarn.

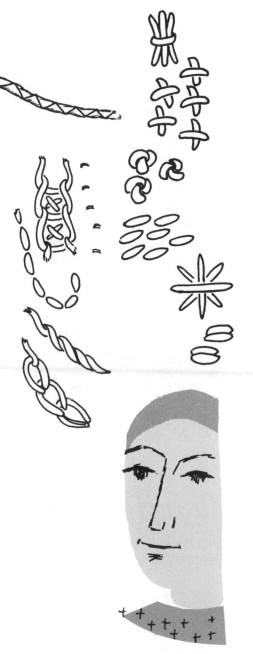

IDEAS
where do they come from?

People ask, "Where do you get your ideas?"
First of all, just as one does not copy when writing a
poem or composing music, one never copies when
designing a banner.

Yes, the same words are used and the same notes, but all
are put together in a different way.

Inspiration may come from the works of other people–
newspaper and magazine ads, Sunday bulletins, greeting cards, the works
of contemporary artists (Picasso, Miró, Léger, Mondrian, Klee,
LaLiberté, Carita), medieval and primitive arts, TV
commercials, packaging, textile designs and from nature and the
world about us. All can be springboards from which design
ideas may come.

Forms from nature might well be the subject matter for a
design, but do not try to reproduce them realistically; rather,
flatten and stylize them (see page 31). Also, it is very
difficult to design with parts of the human body, such as
hands, eyes, and feet.

the theme, the message, the purpose,
the **words**, the *symbols*, the **shapes**,
and the colors—these are your **ideas**

The creative task is **choosing**.
The process is **selecting, sorting,** and **eliminating.**

putting them together

The challenge is how to put the pieces together—how to arrange the unit shapes.
It is like solving a puzzle. *This is designing.*

a SAMPLE design problem

an Easter banner 2' x 4'

1.   Make a list of appropriate words, symbols, or shapes.
2.   Doodle with these. Try soft pencil, felt-tipped pen, marker, or crayon.
3.   Select the **words, symbols,** or **shapes** for this banner. Draw or cut out.
4.   Draw several 1' x 2' rectangles. Measure accurately.
5.   Sketch arrangements in each rectangle, or cut out the words and
        shapes and move them around. Try many. Think about where to
        place and how to space the units.

Three examples:
Choose one.

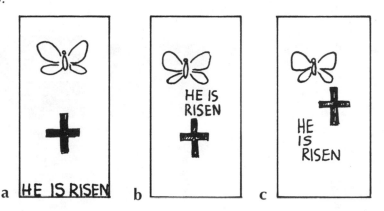

a.   No. The parts are too scattered and the words look as though they
        are a label tacked on the bottom.
b., c. Either of these will work out. Why? The words and symbols fill
        the center of the rectangle. The arrangement is informal enough
        to be joyful in feeling. There is a comfortable margin at the top and
        bottom, and down the sides. The words and symbols are grouped
        together as a unit. See page 41.

the lists:
  ♦ REJOICE
  ♦ CHRIST IS RISEN
  ♦ ALLELUIA
  ♦ VICTORY
  ♦ HE LIVES
  ♦ HE IS RISEN
  ♦ THE LORD IS RISEN, INDEED!

see next page...

just for fun...

See how easy it can be to make the patterns for the designs on the previous page.

Materials:
   three pieces of 9 x 12 construction paper
   in three bright compatible colors
   a piece of chalk,
   a pair of scissors,
   one piece of fabric 2' x 4'.

Draw on the back of the paper with chalk, as large as possible, the shapes indicated in the diagrams. Cut them out, carefully saving the leftover pieces for the decorations on the butterfly and cross.

This design, made at this size in rich fabrics, could be the pattern for an Easter pulpit or lectern hanging.

STYLE *of the design*

Essentially, the two kinds of balance in design—formal and informal—set the style of the banner.

FORMAL

Symmetrical balance is static, formal, traditional. It seems to be the easier, more natural way to work out an arrangement. Formal environment and subject matter sometimes seem to require symmetry. It is what most people mean by balance. When we look in the mirror, we see a symmetrical face!

INFORMAL

Informal or asymmetrical design is also balanced, but the masses of weight are not identical in shape or size and matching, as in a mirror reflection on opposite sides of a centerline. This balance is more subtle, less rigid, more alive.

Both kinds of balance are found in nature.

Below, using the same unit-shapes in the same order, are examples of the two kinds of balance.

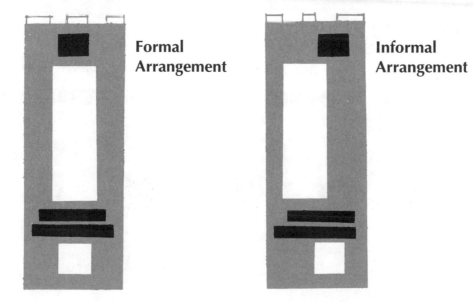

Formal Arrangement

Informal Arrangement

the MESSAGE through DESIGN

Looking at the unit-shapes in the two arrangements on the preceding page, one might ask what these shapes represent.

Actually such shapes will have developed from the shape and size of the symbols, words, and objects that have been chosen as the subject matter of the specific banner.

One warning: Never try to force a symbol, word, or object into a shape that destroys its natural form. Disastrously, letters are often so distorted, for example, an *A* made circular or an *N* triangular.

With this in mind, the top, small rectangle could be:

The large, tall rectangle might represent:

The narrow strips may be words or symbols:

The bottom square could be many things:

42

DESIGNING

SOME HELPS AND HINTS on how to critique your own design

Three poor arrangements:

1. In each, the individual parts of the design are too separated, giving a scattered effect, with no unified center of interest.

2. None has a sufficient margin, i.e., comfortable space around the edges.

3. In each, the four small symbols are too tiny.

4. In *a* and *b*, the words are too spread out and do not seem to be part of the design. In *a* they cut the design in two, and in *b* they appear to be an afterthought. In *c* the words are not considered as a unit and are scattered.

5. In *a*, each symbol's location in a corner prevents any feeling of unity of the parts of the design. Note, this is a formal arrangement.

6. In *b*, the diagonal line of symbols from corner to corner is unpleasant, cuts the design in two, and distorts optically the rectangular shape of the panel. The cross and words are balanced formally, but the symbols informally. This does not work.

7. The top of *c* is informal and the bottom formal, giving a feeling of scattered indecision.

WHAT TO DO

1. Leave margins.
2. Enlarge the four symbols. They need not be all the same size.
3. Decide on either a formal or an informal design.
4. Unify–centralize the arrangement.

These are two possible solutions, but there are many.

more basic arrangements

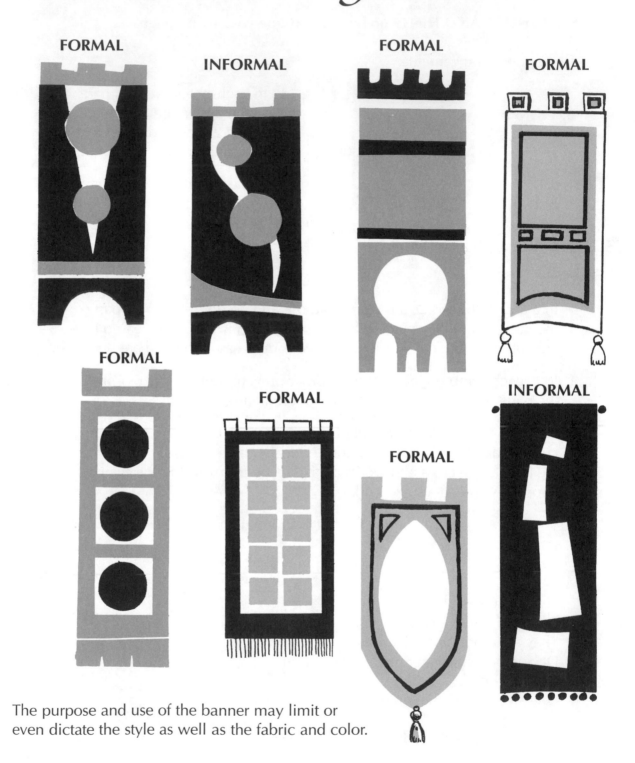

FORMAL   INFORMAL   FORMAL   FORMAL

FORMAL   FORMAL   FORMAL   INFORMAL

The purpose and use of the banner may limit or even dictate the style as well as the fabric and color.

tools and materials

steam iron and press cloth
dressmaker's shears (sharp)
dressmaker's pins
chalk, markers, pen, pencil
dowel stick, ⅝" or ¾" diameter
thread (matching colors and black)
zigzag sewing machine

straightedge (yardstick)
fabric glue
brown wrapping paper
closet pole 6'-8'
fabrics (see page 46)
tracing paper

enlarging the pattern

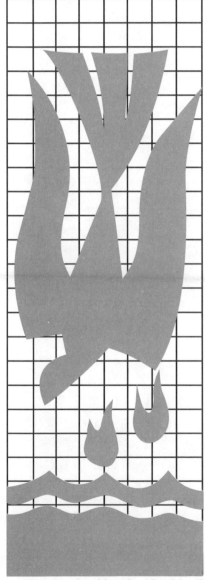

3   6   9   12   15   18   21   24

Decide on **actual finished size** of the banner you plan to make. Cut a piece of brown wrapping paper to the **actual** size of the finished banner. This design is 2' x 6'.

Place a piece of tracing paper on top of your design or on one of the patterns in the book. Carefully trace the outline of the shapes of the banner. A photocopy of the design or pattern will also work.

Measure and mark ½" marks on all four sides of the tracing. If your pattern is small or contains a lot of small detail, your marks may be closer together. Use a ruler and draw lines to connect the marks side to side and up and down to create a ½" **grid** drawn directly on your **copied** pattern or design. Count the squares in your grid across and down.

Now rule your full-sized brown paper into a grid containing the same number of squares as you just counted on your pattern. For example, if your pattern has eight squares across the top and your full-sized brown paper is 24" across, divide 24" by eight and you now know that the grid on your full-sized pattern will be 3". Measure and draw a 3" grid on your full-size brown paper.

Next transfer the design from the small pattern to the brown paper, working one square at a time. This technique will accurately enlarge any design to any size.

A dressmaker's tracing wheel is useful when transferring the parts of the design to **another sheet** of paper to be cut out as patterns.

FABRICS for backgrounds

The fabric for the background must hang with the warp (selvage) up and down in order for the banner to hang right. (See page 47 for amount to purchase.)

- upholstery velvets
- upholstery fabrics, especially textured
- corduroy
- velveteen
- antique satin, especially with slub
- suiting materials
- gabardine
- any firm/rigid cotton-polyester cloth:
    poplin
    duck cloth } also appropriate for linings
    denim

for appliqués

- any of the above
- velour (must be backed, wonderful colors)
- metallic
- suede cloth
- double knits
- any fabric that is the right color
    Turning velvet or corduroy so that the nap goes in opposite directions has the effect of creating a light and dark shade of the same color.

for backing and stiffening

Adhere heavy, nonwoven, fusible interfacing (pelomite) to the back of an ample-sized piece of fabric that is to be used as an appliqué unit. This makes cutting and sewing simpler.

A NOTE ABOUT FELT AND BURLAP
These are recommended *only* for craft, one-time banners, because both fabrics fade and run if wet. They seem out of keeping with the quality of an item that is to be a permanent part of the decor of a church. An exception being the use of natural burlap (sackcloth) in the Lenten season.

MAKING A BANNER

The background color has been chosen (page 34).
The fabric has been selected.

AMOUNT OF FABRIC

To the **actual size** of the banner, add 3" to the width and 12" to the length for seam allowances, casing, and hem when purchasing the background fabric. Purchase two lengths—one for the front and one for the back (see page 46).

appliquéing the DESIGN

1. CHOOSE COLORS IN FABRIC FOR APPLIQUES

Make the final decision on the colors of the **words** and **symbols.** Select these colors in fabric (see page 33).

2. CUT PATTERNS

On heavy brown paper or construction paper, **trace** (from the enlarged design) full-size patterns for each symbol, word, and shape. A dressmaker's tracing wheel is helpful. **Cut** them out.

3. ARRANGE THE DESIGN

Arrange the patterns on the background fabric, within the **actual** size of the finished banner. Remember seam allowances and hem. Stand back, take a look, adjust the patterns until you are satisfied with the design. Now pin or tape them in place.

ABOUT THIS DESIGN:

*It is simple and bold. The symbols and letters are backed with black (see p. 48). The **words** might have been "Jesus Is Lord." See pages 19 and 21 for explanation of the symbols. The background might be bright red velvet; the symbols and letters gold velvet or antique satin. Tiny spots of color could be used within the letters. Or perhaps the background could be bright blue, with off-white letters and symbols. The choices are endless.*

4. PREPARE FABRIC FOR APPLIQUÉS

Almost all fabrics are more easily cut and stitched if they are backed with heavy, nonwoven, fusible interfacing (pelon).

5. CUT OUT APPLIQUÉS

Place paper pattern on backside of fabric, right side of pattern to wrong side of fabric.

Draw around the pattern on the interfacing.

Cut it out and lay it on the background fabric in place of the paper pattern.

6. A RECOMMENDED OPTION

Cut and back an ample piece of **black** fabric as a backing for words, for symbol units or for a figure. Tack and stitch on black, then trim. **Do not** trim too close or evenly (see pages 47, 91, and 108 for examples).

For **figures,** the appliqué units (face, hands, garmets, head covering, etc.) are placed on the black, leaving ample space to separate each unit (see pages 66, 80, and 82 for samples of figures).

7. ADHERING THE DESIGN TO THE BANNER

STITCHING

A small amount of white fabric glue may be used to *tack* the appliqués in place before sewing. The zigzag stitch on the sewing machine will hold appliqués in place and will finish the edges of the cutout. Experiment with the size of the stitch. The thread may be matching, or a complementary or analogous color may add a decorative effect (see page 37).

Tack and sew any decorative shapes on words or symbols before the piece is hitched to the background.

Press the piece before and after stitching.

GLUING

If the design is only to be glued to the background, a thin layer of white, fabric glue over the entire back of the appliqué and close to the edge is the most nearly permanent method. (Gluing is *not* the recommended method.)

MAKING A BANNER

Choose either a casing or tab hangers.

tabs

1. Decide on the number, size, color and shape of the tab hangers.
   Example: five tabs, 5" square, background fabric.

2. Press, then cut out the pieces of fabric. Cut each piece two times as wide as the finished tab and two times as high, plus 2" for seam allowance.

3. Fold longer sides of the fabric to the center, butting the edges. Press.

4. Fold down, matching raw edges. Press.

5" x 5"
finished size
1

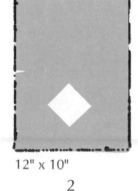

12" x 10"
2

3

4

ATTACHING TABS

Place the raw edges of the tab to the top raw edge of the banner, right sides together, 1½" from the edge or close to the seam allowance of the banner. Pin. Center other tabs and pin in place. Machine baste tabs to banner along the 1" seam allowance.

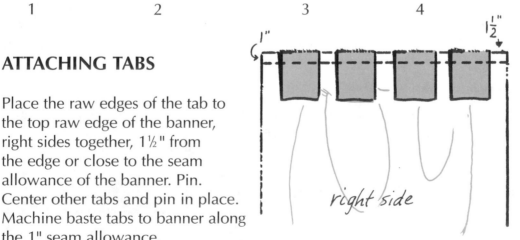

1"

1½"

right side

putting it together

Press the **banners**, both sides, **measure**, and **trim** to straighten the fabric. Stitching the appliqués may have pulled it out of alignment.

A PROCESSIONAL BANNER

If the banner is to be carried, the back side should be of the same fabric as the front. Also, the back side should have some kind of a symbol or design on it, such as a simple cross, chi rho, crown, or descending dove. Even better, the second side could be another banner, perhaps for the same season and interchangeable. NOTE: The reverse side of the banner is seen by the congregation as it is carried down the aisle.

Place the two banners face to face and pin in place. Point pins inward across the seam line, ready for stitching. Stitch from the top on both sides.

A LINED BANNER

If a banner is essentially a **wall hanging,** it will be lined.

Measure
Cut the lining fabric 1" narrower than the background fabric and the same length as the background. Press, (tear to size, if possible), and press again.

Line up
Place right sides together, and line up sides and top of the banner with the lining. Pin in place down both sides of the banner. With the firmer fabric **on the top**, stitch from top to bottom on the two edges.

Press
Press the seams and turn inside out, and press from the lining side both seams to the center. Turn right side out. Set a crease down the sides of the banner. **Always use a press cloth.**

Locate tabs
Turn banner inside out. Locate tabs and pin in place (see page 49). Using a long straight stitch along the 1" seam allowance, sew through the background fabric and the tabs and again through the lining, tabs, and background.

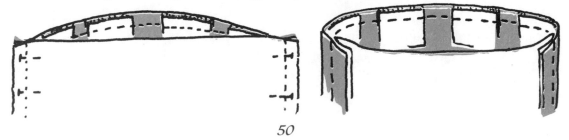

MAKING A BANNER

casing

Leave a couple of inches unstitched
at the top of the side seams for the rod.
Pin along the seam allowance at the top
of the banner, as on the sides. **Stitch** with a long
stitch. Use matching thread. **Press** along the line of
stitching. **Press** the seams open. **Turn inside out**.

The screw eyes, placed 6" apart on center on the
rod, will have to be screwed through the fabric at
the seam line.

the rod

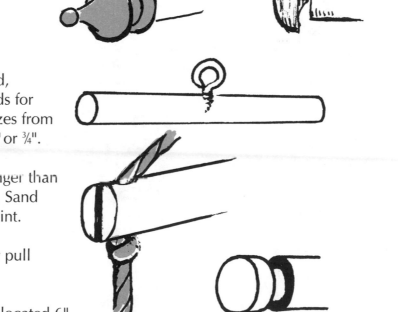

Dowel sticks make good,
inexpensive hanging rods for
banners. Available in sizes from
¼" to 1". Recommend ⅝" or ¾".

Cut the rod about 2" longer than
the width of the banner. Sand
lightly, stain, wax, or paint.

A finial or wood drawer pull
will finish it off.

Two screw eyes will be located 6"
apart on center on the rod.

carrying pole

From the lumberyard, purchase an 8' closet pole. Sand, stain, wax, or paint it. A drapery finial on the top will dress it up.

For an inexpensive pole bracket (hook): **Drill** a hole about 2" from the top through the pole—just big enough to be able to insert a 10" piece of coat-hanger wire. **Center** it and **bend** it down. With pliers, turn up a **hook** at the bottom of each end, from which the screw eyes in the dowel rod will hang.

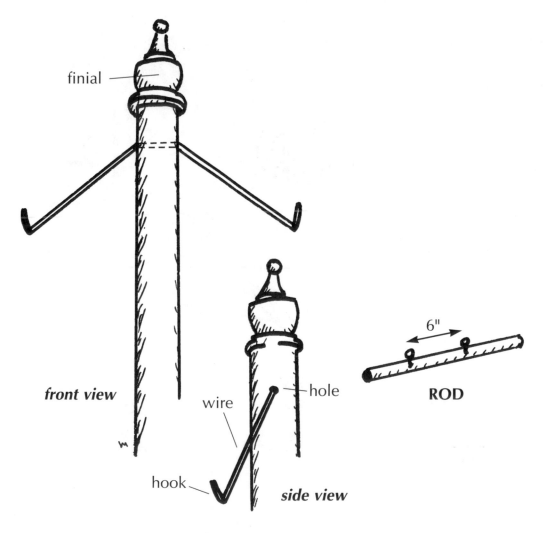

finial

front view

wire

hole

hook

side view

ROD

6"

POLE

TASSELS

1. Wind yarn around a card, box, or book twenty to thirty times.

   Tie at top with a double or triple strand of yarn.

   Remove from the card.

2. Wind yarn several times around the loop to make the top of the tassel. Tie. Using a large needle, run these ends down the center.

   Cut bottom of loop. Trim.

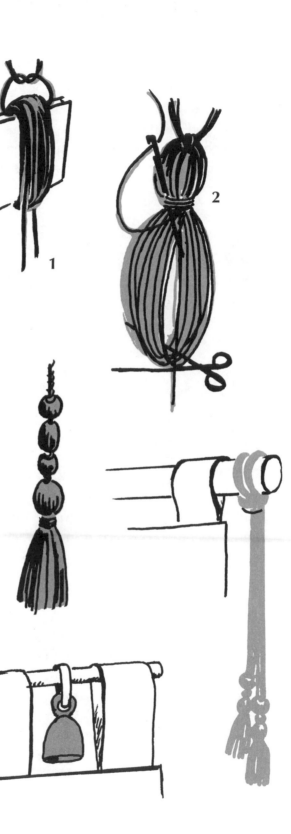

bells

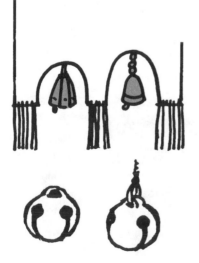

bottom finishings

THE HEM

Turn the banner inside out. Trim excess (bulky) seam allowances at the sides. Hem by hand, using a very large, loose stitch. The bottom is open. A large hem adds weight that makes the banner hang well. If you still have the 10" for the hem, fold it up, press, tuck 5" inside, as in draperies, then stitch by hand.

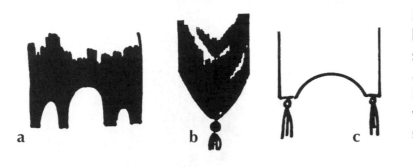

a   b   c

If the shape of the bottom of the banner requires that the lining be stitched to the background, as in *a, b,* and *c,* an opening must be left in the side seam through which the banner is turned right-side out after stitching.

FRINGE

1. Turn a ½" hem on the bottom of the banner. Using a large-eyed needle, thread both cut ends of yarn through the needle. From the back, pull the yarn through the fabric (1) and down through the loop of yarn. Each strand will need to be twice the length of the fringe plus 2" or 3" for looping and trimming. Try two or three strands together, perhaps using two tones of yarn. The fringe may be left ragged or trimmed at the bottom.

2. If the background fabric is coarsely woven material, ravel the bottom from 3" to 12". Sew a line of machine stitching at the place where the raveling is to stop. Make allowance for the additional length of the fringe when measuring and cutting the background fabric. For a heavier fringe, save the ravelings and add them into the raveled fringe, by looping them above the line of stitching, as shown.

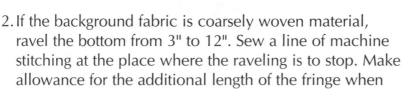

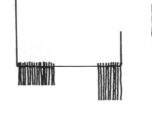

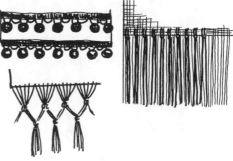

CRAFTS

CHAIN STITCH DESIGN
With chalk, make a line drawing on burlap. Using heavy yarn and an embroidery needle (blunt with large eye), chain stitch along the chalk line. Make a casing at top. Hem or zigzag the sides. Allow length for a raveled fringe.

GIFT-WRAP YARN DESIGN
On a prepared burlap panel, write a word or draw an object with chalk. Squeeze a fine line of white glue along the chalk line and attach the yarn along the glue line.

DESIGN WITH DRAWN THREADS
Pull threads from burlap. Weave in sticks, twigs, wood, metal, yarn, rope, string or pipe cleaners, or tie drawn threads together with yarn, string, or ravelings. Experiment.

CHILDREN'S DRAWINGS
Cut out figures and shapes from an original drawing or painting made by a child. Mount on contrasting paper or colored poster board. Try mounting cutouts on black and recutting, leaving a thick outline before mounting on the background. Words may be added with a colored marker. In order to make your panels rigid at the top so that they hang properly, tack a wood slat across the top back.

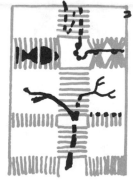

more ways

POSTER BOARD PANELS

1. Cut to a common width (12" to 18" wide) two or three pieces of colored poster board of different heights. On each, paste a paper symbol, word, message, picture, or cut holes in each panel and hang within them symbols made from metal, balsa wood, cardboard, papier mâché, or plastic. To hang, punch holes with paper punch or large needle and string.

2. Glue shapes of bright, light, torn paper to white poster board to make an exciting background for bold, dark designs. A quick method with a professional look.

3. Glue a cut-paper design to heavy poster or matboard. For most interesting effects, have a large selection of colored paper available. Origami and coated art paper comes in brilliant colors. Try overdrawing with heavy lines using a felt marker.

2

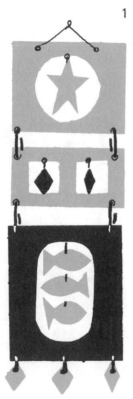

1

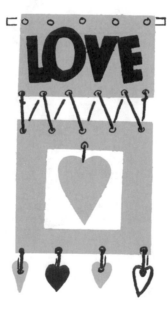

3

BANNERS
with three panels

FAITH, HOPE, AND LOVE
A Thematic Banner

optional width

w

SYMBOLS

♦ Cross = the Christian faith, God's gift of love
♦ Anchor = traditional symbol for hope—well anchored/grounded in the faith
♦ Heart = love; sometimes with a cross, indicating Christian love

COLORS

This hanging might be one of a series, in which case the background of each might be the same. The banner could be gold and the squares in different bright colors, such as bright blue (or blue-green), kelly green, fuchsia (hot pink), orange, or red, on which the symbols could be off-white or even black.

IMPORTANT
When cutting the three panels, add 3" to the length and width of each square to be trimmed to actual size after appliquéing the design.

A CHRISTMAS HANGING

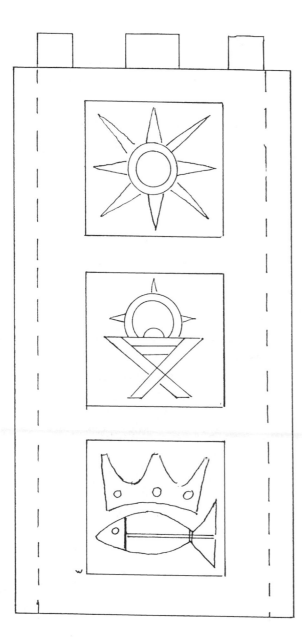

SYMBOLS

- ◆ Decorative star = the Star of Bethlehem
- ◆ Crib = the manger bed
- ◆ Nimbus (halo) with light rays = light of Christ, his divinity
- ◆ Crown = the King has come
- ◆ Fish = Savior or the Savior is born. An ancient acrostic: ichthus (fish), meaning Jesus Christ God's Son Savior

COLORS

The traditional colors for the feast of the Nativity are gold and white. The symbols could be either gold on off-white squares or the reverse. The banner background could be any bright color: red, blue, green, gold, and so forth.

OR

The squares might be a bright color(s) against an off-white banner, and the symbols gold with metallic accents. Make it joyful! Lots of color is a part of the celebration of Christmas.

IMPORTANT

When cutting the three panels, add 3" to the length and width of each square to be trimmed to actual size after appliquéing the design.

AN EASTER HANGING

SYMBOLS

- ♦ IHS = an Iota eta sigma (JES), abbreviation for the word Jesus
- ♦ Sun = the light of heaven
- ♦ Butterfly = the glorified risen body of Jesus. From an apparently dead chrysalis comes the butterfly
- ♦ Words = the Easter message. This could be replaced with another symbol such as a fleur-de-lis, a conventionalized lily.

COLORS

The traditional colors for the Easter season are white and gold, but don't be limited by them. See "A Christmas Hanging" for suggestions.

IMPORTANT
When cutting the three panels, add 3" to the length and width of each square to be trimmed to actual size after appliquéing the design.

BAPTISM AND
HOLY COMMUNION

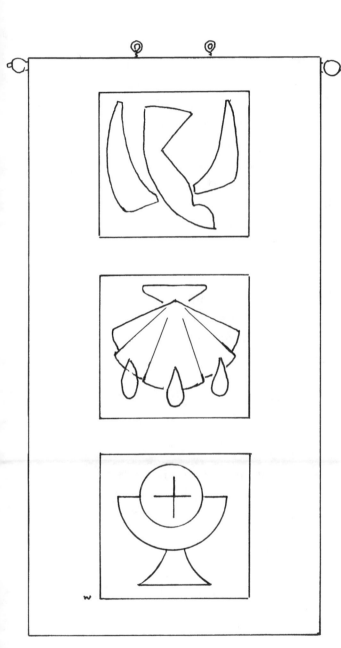

SYMBOLS

- ◆ Descending dove = the blessing of the Holy Spirit
- ◆ Scallop shell = a traditional symbol for baptism
- ◆ Water = the "water of baptism"
- ◆ Three drops = the Holy Trinity
- ◆ Chalice = the cup of salvation, the wine, the blood of Christ
- ◆ Host (bread) = the bread offered by the faithful, the bread of heaven, and the body of Christ

COLORS

The background of the banner could be a rich, medium bright blue. The squares might be gold with white symbols or white with gold symbols. Metallic gold accents on the gold or the white would add a touch of class.

IMPORTANT

When cutting the three panels, add 3" to the length and width of each square to be trimmed to actual size after appliquéing the design.

BREAD OF HEAVEN
Eucharist

SYMBOLS

- Two fish and five loaves = the feeding of the five thousand, prototype of the Holy Eucharist
- Chalice and host = the cup of salvation, the bread of heaven, and the bread and wine offered at the Eucharist
- The words = bread of heaven, from the liturgy

LETTERS

These are letters printed on the computer. They are Optima extra bold, a nice font style. It is sans serif with a slight flare. As printed, they are spaced a little too far apart. When you cut your letters, place them closer together.

COLORS

These symbols and words might be off-white against any bright-colored square. The background of the banner could also be off-white or gold. The squares should be colors that contrast with the banner. The decor of the church building might help you decide.

IMPORTANT

When cutting the three panels, add 3" to the length and width of each square to be trimmed to actual size after appliquéing the design.

HOLY MATRIMONY
A Wedding Banner

SYMBOLS

- ◆ Descending dove = the Holy Spirit of God, who blesses the couple
- ◆ Chi rho = the abbreviation for Christ with two rings = the two individuals being made one through Christ
- ◆ Cross = the Christian symbol meaning love through sacrifice
- ◆ Hearts = love for each other, for God, and for neighbor

COLORS

The traditional colors are gold and white. Off-white symbols in the same or different fabrics would be handsome against a gold square, or reverse it. Accents of metallic fabric, either on the symbols or on the square, could be enriching. Any rich color could be the background of the banner. The location of the banner might determine this.

IMPORTANT
When cutting the three panels, add 3" to the length and width of each square to be trimmed to actual size after appliquéing the design.

THE HOLY TRINITY

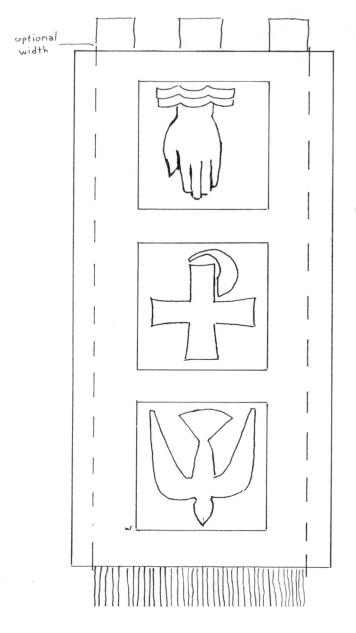

optional width

SYMBOLS

- ♦ Hand reaching down = the hand of God, the Creator, the Father
- ♦ The clouds = the heavens
- ♦ Chi rho = monogram for Christ, God the Son, and Redeemer
- ♦ Descending dove = God the Holy Spirit, sanctifier, and giver of life

COLORS

Traditionally green is associated with the Trinity, so it might be a green banner with gold squares and off-white symbols or any combination of the above. Remember there is no longer a Trinity season, just a Trinity Sunday when gold and white are the recommended liturgical colors.

IMPORTANT
When cutting the three panels, add 3" to the length and width of each square to be trimmed to actual size after appliquéing the design.

BANNERS
with People
Figures

Apostles

Evangelists

Saints

Angels

EVANGELIST

Possibly one of a series of four

ST. MATTHEW

SYMBOL
- The book = Gospel of Matthew
  Cross = a New Testament writing

COLORS
- Background of banner: off-white, neutral tones, or very light gold

THE FIGURE
- Appliquéd on black
- Skin tones: the color of brown wrapping paper
- Coat: red or red-orange
- Trim: possibly a striped fabric of compatible colors
- Hat: gold
- Undergarment: gold
- Trim: another patterned fabric
- Shoes and hair: the black of the background
- Book: black with gold edges and gold cross

LETTERS
- Gold on black. Suggest uncial letters. See pages 17 and 18. Spots of color used the garments, placed within the letters, will make the design more festive.

APPLIQUÉING THE DESIGN
- See pages 47 and 48

ST. MARK

See St. Matthew for more details.

SYMBOL

♦ The book = Gospel of Mark
  Cross = a New Testament writing

COLORS

♦ Background: off-white, neutral
  tones, or very light gold

THE FIGURE

♦ Skin tone: the color of brown
  wrapping paper
♦ Coat: blue-green
♦ Undergarment: light yellow-green
♦ Cap: red-orange
♦ Hair, beard, and feet: the black of
  the background
♦ Book: black with gold edges and
  cross

LETTERS

♦ Gold on black. Suggest uncial
  letters. See pages 17 and 18.

ST. LUKE

See St. Matthew for more details.

SYMBOL

- ♦ The book = Gospel by Luke
  Cross = a New Testament
  writing

COLORS

- ♦ Background: off-white, neutral,
  or very light gold

THE FIGURE

- ♦ Skin tones: the color of brown
  wrapping paper
- ♦ Undergarment: light green or
  yellow-green
- ♦ Drape: two or three reds
- ♦ Hat: red-orange
- ♦ Hair and feet: black of the back-
  ground (see pages 48 and 6)
- ♦ Book: black with gold edges
  and gold cross

LETTERS

- ♦ Gold on black. Perhaps
  uncial letters. See pages
  17 and 18.

ST. JOHN

See St. Matthew for more details.

SYMBOL

- The book = Gospel of John
  Cross = a New Testament writing

COLORS

- Background: off-white, neutral tones, or very light gold

THE FIGURE

- Skin tones: the color of brown wrapping paper
- Undergarment: blue, blue-green, aqua (more than one shade)
- Drape: several shades of gold
- Cap: hot pink
- Hair, beard, and shoes: the black of the background
- Book: black with gold edges and gold cross

LETTERS

- Gold uncial letters are a suggestion. See pages 17 and 18.

ST. PETER
Apostle and Martyr

SYMBOLS (on the shield)
♦ Inverted cross = the means of his martyrdom and/or
♦ crossed keys = symbol of his having been given the "keys of the kingdom." Red background for shield.

COLORS
♦ Background: off-white or natural beige

THE FIGURE
♦ Coat: bright green
♦ Undergarment: lime green (yellow-green)
♦ Shield: orange
♦ Belt: gold
♦ Symbol: black
♦ Skin tones: the color of brown wrapping paper
♦ Hair and beard: the black of the background

NAME
♦ Gold on black

THE OTHER APOSTLES
Follow the above instructions for each of the other apostles, selecting other colors for their clothing and shield. See pages 71 and 72 for the symbols for each of the twelve apostles.

The Apostles' Symbols

ANDREW

ANDREW
The cross saltire, like the letter X, is the shape of the cross on which he was crucified. Blue background.

JAMES

JAMES
Three scallop shells are the symbol of a pilgrim. Red background.

JOHN

JOHN
A chalice from which a serpent rises, carrying the poison by which an attempt was made on his life. Blue background.

MATTHEW

MATTHEW
Three money bags, which refer to his earlier occupation as tax collector. Red background.

THOMAS

THOMAS
A carpenter's square and a spear, which was the instrument of his martyrdom. The square refers to him as a builder of churches. Red background.

BARTHOLOMEW

BARTHOLOMEW
Three flaying knives are a symbol of his martyrdom. Blue background.

The Apostles' Symbols (continued)

SIMON

SIMON
A fish on a book. He is said to be a great fisher of men through the power of the gospel. Red background.

PHILIP
A cross with two circles represents bread from the feeding of the five thousand. Blue background.

PHILIP

JUDE
A sailboat is symbolic of his missionary journeys. Blue background.

JUDE

JAMES THE LESS
A saw was the means of his horrible death. Red background.

JAMES THE LESS

MATTHIAS
A battle-ax refers to his martyrdom, and a book denotes his calling. Red background.

MATTHIAS

The background (field) colors listed above are traditional, and the symbols are always silver (white), gold, or black. Try black symbols (with gold or white accents) on shields of any color that enhances the total design.

Seasonal BANNERS

Advent

Christmas

Epiphany

Lent

Easter

Pentecost

ADVENT
THE LORD IS AT HAND

A formal design (see page 41)

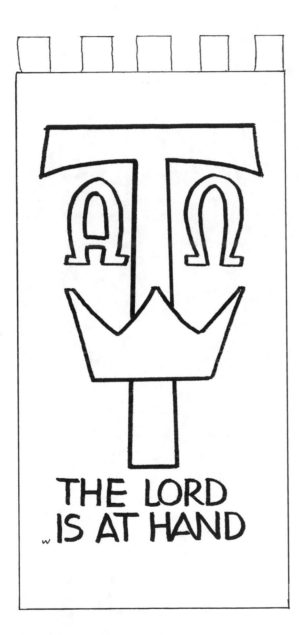

SYMBOLS

♦ Tau cross = the Greek letter tau. This cross form is called the anticipatory cross, the Old Testament cross, or the Advent cross. The staff that Moses held up in the wilderness is often pictured with this cross, with a serpent on it.

♦ Alpha and Omega = first and last letters of the Greek alphabet; Christ is the beginning and the end

♦ Crown = our King and Savior is coming

WORDS

The Lord is at hand. The expectation of the Advent season. Choose uncial letter style. See pages 17 and 18.

COLORS

♦ Background: the traditional colors for the season are either violet or rich blue; therefore, either would be right.

♦ Tau cross and letters: gold or off-white

♦ Alpha and Omega: off-white or gold. Also light, bright pinks or lavenders go well against violet.

HE COMES

SYMBOLS

- ◆ Chi rho = monogram for Christ; Greek letters for CHR
- ◆ Alpha and Omega = Christ, the beginning and the end

WORDS

- ◆ Uncial letter forms. See pages 17 and 18.

COLORS

- ◆ Background: either bright purple or bright blue
- ◆ Chi rho: off-white
- ◆ Letters, Alpha and Omega: gold OR
- ◆ Background: off-white; back all symbols and letters with black. See page 48.
- ◆ Chi rho: bright violet or blue
- ◆ Letters, Alpha and Omega: reverse, bright blue or bright violet

COME, O COME, EMMANUEL

An informal design (see page 41)

SYMBOLS

♦ Four candles = the four Sundays of Advent
♦ Ellipse = the wreath, the circle, which means everlasting life

WORDS

From the ninth-century Latin hymn. The letters are uncial.

COLORS

♦ Background: off-white
♦ Letters: gold mounted on black, as indicated
♦ Candles: lavender (or rose if you wish)
♦ Flames: bright red-orange, yellow-orange, or fuchsia
♦ Ellipse: light pale green

The entire unit mounted on black as indicated. See page 48.

JESSE TREE–Emmanuel, Rejoice

A formal design

SYMBOLS

The family tree of Jesus Christ, through Mary from Jesse, the father of David. See Latin ninth-century hymn "O Come, O Come, Emmanuel."

- ◆ Chi rho: monogram for Christ
- ◆ Monogram: of Mary, virgin
- ◆ Crown: King
- ◆ Sun: Jesus, Son of Righteousness
- ◆ Lamp: wisdom from on high
- ◆ Key: key of David
- ◆ Star of David

WORDS

These are only a suggestion: Emmanuel means "God with us."

COLORS

- ◆ Background: off-white
- ◆ Tree: gold, mounted on black
- ◆ Ornaments: bright violet, bright blue, or fuchsia mounted on black
- ◆ Symbols: black

CHRISTMAS
CHI RHO and CRIB with STAR and CROWN
An informal design

SYMBOLS

- As a whole, this might be titled "The Light coming into the world."
- Chi rho = the Greek letters for CHR, the abbreviation for Christ. In this instance the X form looks almost like beams of light.
- Crib = the manger bed where the baby Jesus lay in the stable
- Halo and rays = the presence of the Christ child
- Crown = the coming of the King
- Star = the Star of Bethlehem
- Lights = stars in the nighttime sky

COLORS

- Background of banner: off-white
- Panel: bright red—a cheerful color for the celebration of the Nativity
- Chi rho and crib: off-white, possibly the same fabric as the background. The crib center is the color of the panel (red). All are backed with black.
- The star, crown, and lights could also be off-white, backed with black, or the crown could be metallic gold; the star, metallic silver; and the lights, silver or pale blue satin, again backed with black.

JOY TO THE WORLD...
An informal design

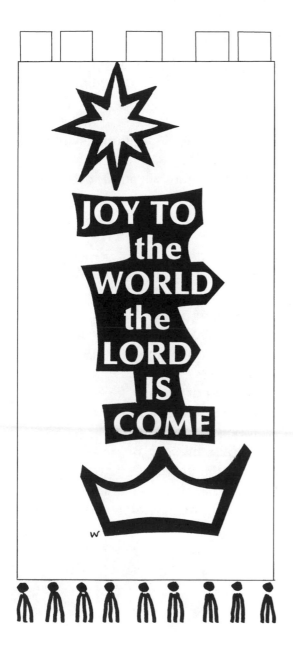

SYMBOLS

- ◆ Star of Bethlehem = the light in the nighttime sky over the manger
- ◆ Crown = "Let earth receive its King"

COLORS

- ◆ Background: bright red or bright blue
- ◆ Letters: either off-white or gold, mounted on black as indicated. Small dabs of color might be placed in the middle of the O's and D's.

   Using uncial letters would enrich the design and make it less mechanical. Uncial letters do not have lowercase letters, therefore the two "the's" would be made slightly smaller in height/scale. See pages 17 and 18.
- ◆ Star and crown: the opposite color from the letters, gold or off-white, mounted on black

MADONNA AND CHILD
Venite adoremus

SYMBOLS

- Crown = St. Mary wears a crown indicating that she is queen of heaven
- Halo = light, holiness
- Christmas rose = traditional symbol for Christmas
- Venite adoremus = Latin for "Come Adore"

COLORS

- Background: bright red or medium bright blue (or gold, or off-white)
- Figure, letters, and rose: all mounted on black
- Mary: blue or pink robe, white dress, and gold or white crown
- Jesus: white
- Halo: gold or metallic
- Skin tones: the color of brown wrapping paper
- Rose: off-white or rose
- Leaves: soft green
- Letters: gold or off-white on the black, perhaps uncial. See pages 17 and 18.

MADONNA AND CHILD
Joyful Tidings, Jesus Is Born

SYMBOLS
- St. Mary holding the Christ child
- Nimbus (halo) = for Jesus, the cruciform rays mean divinity; for Mary the plain halo means sainthood.

COLORS
- Traditionally, Mary wears blue, but pink and white and touches of gold are appropriate.
- Infant Jesus: wrapped in white
- Halos: any color. Gold (metallic) is traditional; white can be used. Whatever balances the color of the design will be right.
- Background of banner: medium bright blue or bright red.
- Letters: gold velvet against black.

THE ANGEL
Glory to God on High or Peace on Earth

SYMBOL

The Angel of the Lord. He is not described in Scriptures, but he is *not* a pretty lady or little child! He is a messenger of God.

♦ Nimbus (halo) = light and holiness

COLORS

♦ In medieval paintings, angels are robed in brilliant colors, richly decorated. The wings are as colorful as the most exotic birds. There is also lots of gold!

♦ If you are daring, the background might be off-white; however, gold is an option. If you prefer a paler angel, you will want a bright background, red or blue.

♦ Skin tone: the color of brown wrapping paper

♦ Halo: any bright color, gold, or off-white

♦ Letters: these should be backed with black just as the figure is. Any color that *contrasts* strongly with the black and picks up a color in the wings or robe of the angel will balance the design.

EPIPHANY
THREE CROWNS

A formal design

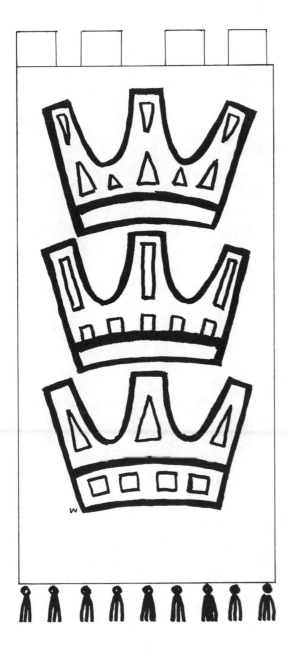

SYMBOLS
- Three crowns = the Three Magi, Wise Men, Kings

COLORS
- Background: off-white, red, or some other bright color
- Crowns: gold, with jewels of many bright color The crowns are mounted on black to accent their brilliance. See page 48.

EPIPHANY MISSION
Go Forth

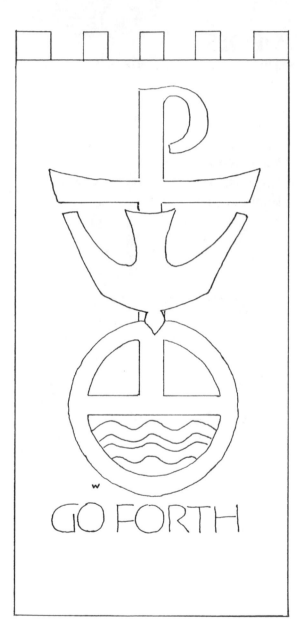

The theme of this design is appropriate for many occasions: baptisms, confirmations, ordinations, commissioning lay ministers, and so on.

SYMBOLS

- Descending dove = the Holy Spirit
- The chi rho on the orb = Christ's reign over the world
- Water = "Go into all the world and baptize through the power of the Spirit."

LETTERS

Bold caps, spaced close together. See page 10 ff. or 17–18.

COLORS

- Background: red (vermilion, scarlet, crimson, cranberry) or whatever looks best in the building. Reds do not have to match.
- Chi rho and orb: off-white
- Water: gold or blue/blue-green
- Dove and letters: gold

All are mounted on black. See page 48.

EPIPHANY—HOLY BAPTISM

An informal design

SYMBOLS

- Descending dove = the Holy Spirit
- Scallop shell = traditional symbol for baptism
- Three drops of water = the water of baptism and the Holy Trinity, in whose name the baptism is performed
- Water = Holy Baptism

COLORS

- Background: medium bright blue
- Dove: off-white and maybe a little pink in a wing and tail feather
- Shell: shell pinks and off-white
- Three drops: pale blue-greens
- Water: two shades of light blue

All are mounted on black.

BAPTISM
One Lord, One Faith, One Baptism
An informal design

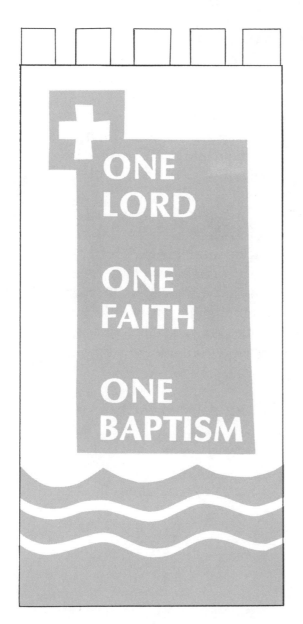

SYMBOLS

- ◆ Cross = we are signed with a cross at baptism. The cross is *the* Christian symbol. At baptism one is made a Christian.
- ◆ Water = washing, cleansing. It is essential for life.

LETTERS

The use of uncial letters will make this design less sterile. See pages 17 and 18.

COLORS

If this banner is used as the second side of a baptismal banner, the color of the background will match the other side. Same color, same fabric.

- ◆ Background: gold
- ◆ Water: bright blue, perhaps two or three shades
- ◆ Words: off-white against black, blues in center of *O*'s, *D*'s, and so on
- ◆ Cross: light blue against black

LENT—HOLY WEEK
Three Crosses

A formal design

SYMBOLS

- Three crosses = Calvary. Traditionally, the thieves' crosses are tau crosses.
- Crown of thorns = suffering of Jesus
- INRI = the sign placed on the cross: Jesus of Nazareth, King of the Jews (the R = Rex)

COLORS

- Background: color of sackcloth or burlap
- Center cross: black
- Two tau crosses: dark, dried-blood red
- INRI: black
- Crown of thorns: blood red
- Ground: black

LENT—PALM SUNDAY
Hosanna
An informal design

SYMBOLS
- ◆ Star of David = Jesus is called the Son of David
- ◆ Crown = Jesus is hailed as the King
- ◆ Palm branches = the branches that were waved to greet the King

WORDS
Hosanna, to the King

COLORS
- ◆ Background: sackcloth or a dark off-white (oatmeal)
- ◆ Star: blue
- ◆ Palm branch: green
- ◆ Crown: gold
- ◆ Hosanna: bright red or fuchsia
- ◆ All units against black. See page 48.

EASTER

ALLELUIA, CHRIST IS RISEN

A formal design

SYMBOLS

- Circle of the Celtic cross = the eternal nature of the Resurrection
- Empty cross = Jesus is risen; he no longer hangs on it
- Five triangles = the five wounds of Christ (also decorative)

COLORS

- Background: off-white (the liturgical color for Easter) or light bright blue
- Cross: backed with black, might be gold velvet on gold satin, and the triangles metallic
- Circle: metallic gold
- The letters: gold against black or olive green. Try uncial letter forms. See pages 17–18.

THE LORD IS RISEN
With Cross, Lilies, and Butterfly
An informal design

SYMBOLS

- ♦ Empty cross = resurrection
- ♦ Lily = a traditional Easter symbol
- ♦ Butterfly = resurrection/new life. From the apparently dead chrysalis comes the new life.

COLORS

- ♦ Background: off-white (the traditional color for Easter) or gold
- ♦ Cross: gold against black, or off-white
- ♦ Lily: white; olive green leaves and stem, and gold stamens
- ♦ Butterflies: gold with green or bright decorations

LETTERS

Gold, with centers of the same bright colors, against black. Uncial letters would enrich this design. See pages 17 and 18.

BEHOLD THE LAMB OF GOD— THE AGNUS DEI

An informal design

SYMBOLS

- Lamb = A triradiant nimbus signifies the lamb as a member of the Trinity. The lamb was a sacrificial animal.
- Banner = Jesus' triumph over death, his resurrection.

WORDS

Behold the Lamb of God. John the Baptist pointed to Jesus as the Lamb of God.

COLORS

- Background: medium blue
- Lamb: off-white
- Nimbus: gold or many colors
- Rays: white or metallic
- Staff and cross: gold
- Flag: white with red cross
- All mounted on black
- Letters: gold or off-white against black. Dabs of color within the letters.

CHI RHO WITH CROWN

A formal design

CHRIST THE KING

SYMBOLS

- ♦ Chi rho with cross = the Greek letters X (CH) and Rho (R); the monogram for Christ, with the horizontal line making a cross
- ♦ Crown = Christ reigns with the Father

WORDS

Other options include Jesus is King, He lives, Jesus is Lord, Christ is risen, He is risen, Rejoice, or Alleluia.

The words "Christ the King" make the banner appropriate for the Sunday before Advent.

COLORS

- ♦ Background: red
- ♦ Panel on the background: off-white
- ♦ Crown: gold
- ♦ Chi rho: red

HE IS RISEN, ALLELUIA
With Butterfly and Fleur-de-lis
An informal design

SYMBOLS

♦ Butterfly = resurrection, new life. From an apparently lifeless chrysalis comes the new life, the life resurrected from the grave, a glorious body prepared for eternity.

♦ Fleur-de-lis = a lily in a conventionalized form. Because the lily blooms at Easter time, it has become the Easter flower. Also, it grows from a seemingly dead bulb.

WORDS

He is risen, Christ is risen, or the Lord is risen—all are the good news of Easter the message of Easter.

LETTERS

These are uncial letters.

COLORS

♦ Background: off-white, the traditional color for the Easter season

♦ Letters: gold against black or dark olive green. Decorate the centers of the letters with the colors used in the butterfly. See page 91.

♦ Butterfly: gold (the two sides do not have to be the same fabric). The spots of color may be bright colors—pink, blue, orange, or lavender. Play with the shapes and colors. Place all against black or green.

♦ Fleur-de-lis: like the butterfly, gold against black or green

PENTECOST
COME HOLY SPIRIT

An informal design

SYMBOLS

- ◆ Descending dove = the Holy Spirit (Mark 1:10)
- ◆ Flames/tongues of fire = the Holy Spirit (Acts 2:3)

COLORS

- ◆ Background: gold
- ◆ Dove: red with orange, gold, or pink accents
- ◆ Flames: red, orange, fuchsia, and pink
- ◆ Letters: a darker gold or red, orange, or fuchsia

DESCENDING DOVE

An informal design

SYMBOLS

- ◆ Descending dove = the Holy Spirit coming
- ◆ Flames = the tongues of fire that came upon the disciples on the day of Pentecost (Acts 2:3)

COLORS

- ◆ Background: off-white or gold
- ◆ Dove and flames: red, fuchsia, orange against black
  OR
- ◆ Background: red
- ◆ Dove and flames: off-white (different textures) and gold metallic accents, all against black

COME HOLY SPIRIT, FILL OUR HEARTS

An informal design

SYMBOL

- ♦ Flames/tongues of fire = the gifts of the Holy Spirit that came upon the apostles at Pentecost (Acts 2:3)

COLORS

- ♦ Background: red
- ♦ Flames: gold or off-white on black
- ♦ Flame centers: red, red-orange, or orange

LETTERS

This is the alphabet of lower-case letters seen on page 17; off-white on black or gold on black. Centers of the *O's*, *P*, and *A* might pick up the color of the flame centers.

COME HOLY SPIRIT, FILL OUR HEARTS
With Four Flames
An informal design

SYMBOLS

♦ Flames = the tongues of fire that came upon the apostles on the day of Pentecost (Acts 2:3)

WORDS

This might be more beautiful if uncial letters were used. See pages 17, 18, and 91.

COLORS

♦ Background: red, red-orange, or fuchsia

♦ Flames: off-white and gold with touches of metallic, or reverse the colors

TRINITY
HOLY TRINITY
Three Circles and a Triangle
A formal design

HOLY TRINITY

SYMBOLS

- Triangle = the equilateral triangle has three equal sides, an obvious symbol for the Trinity
- Three circles = three circles intertwined indicate the unity of the three persons of the Holy Trinity. To draw the enlarged circles, use a string with a pin at one end and a pencil or a piece chalk as the marker.

COLORS

- Background: off-white or a neutral
- Triangle and circles: four different shades of green. Perhaps the triangle might be a darker green. Place all against gold.
- Letters: a green, backed against gold

THREE FISH IN A TRIANGLE
Trinity Church
A formal design

SYMBOLS

- Fish = probably the earliest Christian symbol is the fish. The Greek word ichthus became an acrostic for the words: Jesus Christ God's Son Savior. Three is the number for the Holy Trinity.

WORDS

Many churches, schools, and institutions are called by this name. Also, Trinity Sunday is the Sunday after the Feast of Pentecost.

COLORS

Traditionally, green has been associated with the Trinity, but there is no longer a Trinity season, which allows for a wider use of color.

- Background: off-white, gold, neutral, light green, or bright green
- Fish: The three might be of three different shades of green of the same value; for example, green, blue-green, yellow-green, and aqua. The heads could be another shade, or the line down the center could divide the body into two colors, all divided by black.

THREE FISH, A TRIANGLE, AND CIRCLE
Trinity School

SYMBOLS

- Three fish = the number of the Holy Trinity
- Equilateral triangle = three equal sides
- Circle = one endless line; therefore, it is symbolic of the oneness of the persons of the Holy Trinity. Unity in Trinity.

COLORS

See previous page for suggestions.

- Background: green, gold, off-white, or light green
- Fish: gold
- Triangle and circle: dark/bright green
- Center of circle: the background color
- Letters: same as fish, against black or dark green

ALL SAINTS' BANNER
Cross and Crowns
A formal design

SYMBOLS

- Crowns = those who have been awarded crowns—the saints
- Cross = a life in Christ the Savior

COLORS

The liturgical color for the Feast of All Saints is gold or white. The symbols and letters might be gold placed against red, the color of martyrs, or any color that will enhance the decor of the church.

LETTERS

Uncial letter forms. See page 18.

Thematic
BANNERS

WEDDING BANNER—
CROSS WITH FOUR HEARTS
A formal design

SYMBOLS

- Cross = God's love, *the* Christian symbol, Christian marriage
- Hearts = love. Here it could imply the love of the two to be joined in Holy Matrimony, the love of the community or family, and the love of God. Note that the hearts are not all alike.

COLORS

- Background: a color appropriate for the building, such as bright blue or red
- Cross: gold
- Hearts: a variety of golds accented with burnt orange, chartreuse, or other related colors
  OR
- Background: off white
- Cross and Hearts: a bright color; several shades in the hearts—experiment.
- All against black

CHI RHO WITH TWO RINGS
A formal design

SYMBOLS

- Chi rho = the Greek letters for Christ, modified to be a cross form
- Two rings = the two people to be united in Holy Matrimony

COLORS

- Background: off-white
- The Chi rho/cross = metallic gold
- The two rings: gold fabric—two kinds; two shades for the two individuals
  OR
- Choose shades of red (pink), green, blue for the symbols

WEDDING BANNER

A formal design

SYMBOLS

- Chi rho = Christ; the Greek letters for Christ, His monogram
- Two rings = the two people who come to be joined in Holy Matrimony. The union of husband and wife in heart, body, and mind.

COLORS

- Background: off-white
- Chi rho: red/pinks, blues, or greens. The chi (X) may be on top of the rho and a slightly different shade of the same color. Accents may be gold or metallic gold.
- Two interlocking circles: The two circles will be shades of the color of the chi rho. They will be different from each other, because they represent two different people whose lives are coming together. Note the lines indicating a change of fabric/shade. Gold accents might enrich the design. Outline all the shapes with a black backing or other contrasting color that will tie the parts together.

Alternate suggestion:
- Background: a medium color (the building or the bride's colors may be the determining factor.)
- Design: gold and off-white against black backing

DOVE AND TWO ENTWINED HEARTS
We Are One in the Lord

SYMBOLS

- ◆ Descending dove = the Spirit of God coming down on the two to be joined in Holy Matrimony
- ◆ Two hearts = the two to be joined

COLORS

If this is the back of another banner, it will be the same color and fabric as the other side. See Chi rho with Two Rings.

The accent pieces on the dove and hearts may be metallic or a shade of the actual color of the symbol. They represent flames of fire of the Holy Spirit.

LETTERS

The same light color as the symbols, or possibly gold. All against black.

The banner might simply read "One in the Lord." Uncial letters will make it more handsome. See pages 17, 18, and 91.

THEMATIC
CHRIST, KING, SAVIOR

SYMBOLS

- ◆ Chi rho = Christ; Greek letters for Christ, his monogram
- ◆ Crown = Lord, King
- ◆ Fish = the acrostic from ichthus, meaning Jesus Christ God's Son Savior.

COLORS

The effect is that of a stained-glass window.

- ◆ Background: gold or bright blue, or blue-green
- ◆ Chi rho: four or five different golds in different fabrics; straight through the fish and crown
- ◆ Crown: some golds for the points, one yellow-orange. The bottom squares off-white, blue, blue-green, and yellow-green.
- ◆ Fish—tail, body, and head: blue-green, blue of different fabrics
- ◆ Eye: off-white

All mounted on black.
Suggestion: Leave an entire black panel behind the whole design (see drawing).

THY KINGDOM COME

A formal design

SYMBOLS

- Chi rho = the Greek letters X (CH) and Rho (R), the monogram for Christ.
- Alpha and Omega = the first and last letters in the Greek alphabet
- Crown = Christ reigns in the kingdom of God

WORDS

From the Lord's Prayer

COLORS

- Background: red
- Chi rho and Alpha and Omega: gold, all against black
- Crown: gold or off-white with red jewels

LETTERS

Gold or off-white with spots of red or other bright color, or metallic within the round letters, against black. These are uncial letters.

THE WORD

A formal design

THE
WORD

SYMBOLS

- ◆ Chi rho = Greek letters for Christ's monogram. Jesus Christ is the Logos, the Word (John 1:1).
- ◆ Book = the Holy Bible. The Scriptures are called the Word of God.

COLORS

- ◆ Background: red or bright blue
- ◆ Chi rho: gold, outlined with black
- ◆ Book: pages off-white; edges gold; binding black
- ◆ Letters: gold against black

I AM THE VINE

An informal design

I AM THE VINE

SYMBOLS and WORDS

- ♦ Vine and branches = Jesus said, "I am the vine, and you are the branches" (John 15:5).
- ♦ Also The Tree of Life (Genesis 2:9–10, Revelation 22:1–5)

COLORS

- ♦ Background: rich medium blue
- ♦ Trunk and branches: gold and light yellow-green
- ♦ Leaves: yellow-green, yellow-orange, light olive, and salmon

All are mounted on black

LETTERS

Gold or one of the leaf colors mounted on a black strip which becomes the bottom edge of the banner.

Morehouse Publishing
P.O. Box 1321
Harrisburg, PA 17105

Morehouse Publishing is a division of The Morehouse Group.

Cover design by Corey Kent and Kirk Bingaman

Library of Congress Cataloging-in-Publication Data

Wolfe, Betty.
    The new banner book / Betty Wolfe
      p. cm.
    ISBN 0-8192-1781-6 (pbk.)
    1. Church pennants. I. Title
  BV168.F5W65 1998
  246'.55—dc21   98-23426
                                 CIP

Printed in the United States of America

03 02 01 00 99 98   10 9 8 7 6 5 4 3 2 1